THE BOOK OF MALACHI

Adventures of an Ethiopian Adoptee and his TV News Dad

Jay Siltzer

The Book of Malachi
Adventures of an Ethiopian Adoptee and his TV News Dad

Grateful acknowledgement is made for photo permission from the following: Asheville Regional Airport, pg. 8; Estee Felten, pg. 12; back cover photo, WLOS-TV.

All other photos are from the Siltzer family.

All individual postings previously appeared on Facebook Jay Siltzer or Jay Siltzer WLOS 2011-2015.

Published by CreateSpace, an Amazon company

DEDICATION

This book is dedicated to the memory of
Kelly McKeown Siltzer 1968-2014

TABLE OF CONTENTS

INTRODUCTION

There are a few things to keep in mind for the quips and quotes in this book to make sense. First, my wife, Kelly, and I adopted Malachi from Ethiopia in 2009, when he was only a year old. Secondly, Kelly died in 2014 from a rare form of leukemia. Finally, Malachi is battling his own health issues, including a brain tumor.

Please, though, don't feel sorry for any of us. This book is not about sorrow, but rather the joy and laughter that arise from everyday life. Malachi has brought me unending happiness through his outrageousness – more craziness than I've experienced in 25 years of news reporting. (Some of those stories are included, too.) I began compiling my son's antics and posting them on Facebook a few years ago. This book is a collection of those moments, often verbal exchanges between him and me.

You can read the book cover to cover, or you can flip through it randomly. It doesn't matter. What I hope you take away is that I couldn't be more proud of my Ethiopian-born son who despite adversity lives each day to laugh.

CONVERSATIONS

"You have nice, thick hair," I told Malachi while picking out the tangles following his bath the other night.

"You don't," my 5-year-old son responded. "You have a hole in your head."

I snapped back, "I needed that comment like I needed another hole in the head!"

December 15, 2014

Malachi and I are moving to a new home locally that requires less upkeep. Yesterday, we met the buyers of our current home.

"Dad, tell them about the bears!" Malachi shouted.

"I'm trying to sell the house," I replied in disbelief. "Don't scare them (the buyers) away."

(By the way, two cubs walked through my yard last year; it doesn't really matter that one chased me around my car.)

October 14, 2011

I've been talking to schoolchildren all week about weather, but I've been the one dodging the storms.

Yesterday, a youngster asked me if I have children. I told the student I have a son who is three.

After inquiring about my age, the third grader responded, "Wow, you're a lot older than my mom and dad... and your kid is only three!"

Thanks for the reminder. Glad something in my weather presentation blew you away.

November 3, 2014

Getting ready for church on All Saints' Sunday and All Souls' Day proved challenging.

"Malachi, get your shirt and pants on," I repeated, only to be followed by a response as indiscernible as Charlie Brown's teacher.

"Dude, I can't understand that gibberish," I said. "Is English your second language?" Without missing a beat, my 6-year-old son replied, "Yes, yes it is. Ethiopian was my first language."

I'm getting a white flag to wave the international sign of surrender.

September 22, 2013

"Did I win?" Malachi asked after completing the
Runway 5K at Asheville Regional Airport on Saturday.

"You were the youngest person to finish," I told my 5-
year-old son, complimenting his finish time of 40
minutes.

"What did I win?" Malachi continued with great
expectation.

"How about a trip to Chick-fil-A?" I offered.
Malachi put his chin down, "I was hoping for more."

October 28, 2014

While registering for a 5K run, my son questioned,
"Should I tell them I'm Ethiopian? That way they'll
know I'm fast."

"Malachi, there are 4,000 people here," I replied. "You
aren't going to win."

December 17, 2011

My child one-upped me at dinner last night. We went to
Cracker Barrel after church; he ordered pancakes, an egg
and biscuit. But, when the food came, he didn't touch it.

"Why aren't you eating?" I asked in frustration.
Malachi responded, "...because I ate at school and had
snacks at church."

"Then, why order this?" I asked.
"So we can take it home for tomorrow," my 3-year-old
menu planner replied. That's exactly what we did.

August 25, 2014

We went to a friend's house for a party Saturday night
and a tall, middle-aged blonde answered the door.

"Are you Diane Sawyer?" asked a wide-eyed Malachi.
"No," she replied, "but you are now my favorite."

<u>July 24, 2013</u>

Watching an episode of PBS' "Sid the Science Kid" with Malachi seemed harmless enough the other night until he saw the light.

The episode centered on "light sources," including the sun, light bulbs, and vehicle headlights.

"Malachi, can you name other light sources?" I asked.

My 5-year-old son too eagerly replied, "...the moon, lightning bugs, and the top of your head, Daddy."

<u>June 3, 2013</u>

"Saying 'Hey, brown man like me!' is not the best way to summon your server at a restaurant," I told Malachi.

"He is brown," my child replied.

<u>June 3, 2013</u>

"Telling the priest at school you were born in Ethiopia was great," I explained to Malachi. "But, why in the world did you tell him you pooped on me on the flight to America?"

Looking perplexed, my 5-year-old son replied, "...because it's true."

March 6, 2013

I recently told Malachi that years ago my dad won a trivia contest only to discover that his prize -- a big bag of Hershey's Kisses -- was filled with worms.

My son thought it was hilarious, and I did, too, until last night. At the end of our meal at a local restaurant, the server brought the check and left three Kisses.

"No thank you," Malachi said. "I think they have worms in them!" I offered no explanation, left a good tip, and inched my way quietly toward the door.

May 26, 2015

"I've decided what I'm going to do," Malachi notified me. "I want to be a magician when I grow up."

Instead of rolling my eyes, I told him that was great and he could major in speech and theater in college.

"That way you can be a performer and learn how to sing, tell jokes, and play an instrument," I said. "You might even use that degree to become a newsman."

Malachi replied, "No, I don't want to wake up my kids (so early) every morning while getting ready."

November 15, 2012

My invitation to Malachi to join me and co-anchor Holly Headrick in The Asheville Holiday Parade on Saturday has been met with nothing but questions.

"Do I have to walk?" my 4-year-old son asked, somewhat skeptical of participating. "No," I replied. "We will be sitting up on the back of a convertible."

He thought for a minute, "Will I have a seat belt?"

"No, we won't be going fast," I answered. "It's the one time you won't have to wear a seat belt."

Malachi followed up, "What if the policeman stops us?" I responded in exhaustion, "I'm sure you will talk your way out of the situation by blaming me."

December 21, 2011

Malachi and I made a stop for a Christmas gift yesterday when I parked next to a car with "antlers."

Malachi asked if it was Rudolph's car.

"Probably," I answered without thinking. Then, my 3-year-old began looking at the driver in the car. (She literally had a red nose -- perhaps from inebriation, rosacea, or some other condition.)

Malachi yelled, "Daddy, it's Mrs. Rudolph; I want to go talk to her!" I told him she was busy and moved our car to the other side of the parking lot.

September 23, 2015

Last night's dinner conversation after a rough day...

Mimi (Malachi's paternal grandmother): "If we had a reality show, no one would believe it."

Malachi: "Yeah, my friends wouldn't watch it."

Jay: "You're right; that's because they're living it with you."

Malachi: silence... followed by a growling sound.

September 8, 2015

Discussing school took an unexpected turn.
"My girlfriend says she hates me," Malachi declared.
"I'm sorry," I replied. "I guess it's time to move on."
Malachi shook his head, "No, she's just playing it cool."

March 20, 2014

Malachi told me he was writing a story to share at
school. Seconds later, he asked me how to spell "hit."
Skeptically, I offered h-i-t. A few minutes later, he read,
"Jay hit Malachi, bomb, boom, boom!"

"What kind of story is that?" I asked, impressed he could
spell bomb and boom. "It's not true," I added.

Malachi replied, "I know, but it's funny."
"It's not going to be funny when DSS is knocking at my
door," I responded in frustration. "You're not taking that
to school. Write another story!"

November 25, 2013

Malachi's weekend cough caught me by surprise.
"Quit that," I said of my 5-year-old son's hacking and
snorting. "I need my voice and don't want to catch that."
Malachi instantly replied, "Daddy, if you get it, you'll
sound like a pig. People will still watch; they'll just
laugh."

January 22, 2015

Dinner proved cheesy last night.
"What is this?" Malachi asked of the green and orange concoction on his plate.
"It is broccoli and cheese," I replied as my 6-year-old son tried it.
"It would be better without the broccoli," he remarked.
"I know," I responded. "Eat it anyway."

January 13, 2014

While running with my 5-year-old son at Fletcher Park yesterday afternoon, he suddenly yelled, "Snake!"

There was no snake, just a partially buried cord in the mud and several relieved walkers.

"Dude, you just panicked the public," I told Malachi. Then, I thought for a minute; that's what I do all the time. Like father, like son, I guess.

June 29, 2015

"The Empire 'Struck' Back" at me while watching the Star Wars movie with Malachi for the first time.
"Daddy, he's like you," my 7-year-old son said of C-3PO. "What do you mean?" I asked.
"He sounds like you," Malachi answered, and then continued with additional comparisons. "He's crazy and wants everything perfect like you."
May the force be with me.

January 7, 2012

I think I will get Malachi a metal detector for his upcoming birthday. He recently returned from my in-laws' house with a Ziploc bag filled with coins.

"What's this?" I asked.
Malachi responded, "It's money. I found it in Andma's couch."

I could not have been more proud. I began thinking; if he begins scanning the beach at 8 a.m., then he might pay for a week's trip in only a couple of days.

November 19, 2012

My recent lessons for Malachi centering on "good decisions" and "bad decisions" have boomeranged.

Yesterday morning, my 4-year-old son awakened me and proclaimed, "Daddy, the policeman is coming to arrest you!" Perplexed, I asked, "Why?"

"You bought a cold, old house," Malachi answered, pretending to shiver. "That was a bad decision."

"Yes, yes it was," I responded.
Perhaps calling the HVAC repairman today will be a good decision.

February 24, 2013

Oscar party has taken on a whole new meaning at our house.
"Can we have a grouch party?" 5-year-old Malachi asked earlier today.
"What are you talking about?" I questioned, failing to immediately associate an Oscar party with "Sesame Street's" Oscar the Grouch.
"It's his birthday," Malachi said of the Muppet.
"Yes, we can have an Oscar party," I laughed. "Who better to foot the bill for a grouch party than another grouch?"

October 7, 2013

Five-year-old Malachi sensed my frustration installing mini blinds and questioned me.
"Daddy, did you fight in a war?" he asked.
"No," I replied.
"I'm glad you weren't in a war," Malachi continued.
"You would have turned the cannon over and shot your foot."

December 22, 2013

"Malachi, I need to stop at the medicine store before we go home," I told my child. My son questioned, "Isn't it supposed to say C-V-S, not A-B-C?"

December 9, 2014

"There are kids at my school who have squirrel teeth," Malachi told me last night, explaining their two front permanent upper teeth have come in.

"You're one to talk, Mike Tyson," I replied.

"Who's he?" Malachi asked.

"A boxer with no front teeth like you," I replied.

"Is he a nice guy?" Malachi continued.
Ask the guy without an ear!

January 27, 2012

Malachi knocked off a baseboard heat cover in our old house and discovered splatters of pink paint. I explained to him the eccentric woman who lived there years ago liked that color.

"My room was PINK?" Malachi asked in disgust.

"Yes," I responded. "The entire house was pink until it was repainted." My child covered his ears and began running through the house, yelling, "I don't want to live in a girl's house!" John Cougar liked "Pink Houses" a lot more than Malachi.

March 21, 2012

Here is how a simple statement to my son resulted in my loss of self-esteem.

Jay: "Malachi, you need to go to the doctor for your 4-year checkup."
Malachi: "No, Daddy, you need to go to the doctor to get some hair for your circle."
Jay: "I'm glad you have a full head of hair; I just wish you had some tact."

July 21, 2014

The hardest thing I have ever done is tell Malachi that his mother and my wife, Kelly, died. I took him to a local cemetery and we read several tombstones.

"There's a cross on that one," my son said of one marker while moving to another. "There is a flag on that one. Maybe he was a soldier."

I then asked Malachi why I brought him there. He immediately made the connection to Kelly's death and burst into tears.

"I knew in my heart this was going to happen," my 6-year-old said. Then, he remembered his mom's culinary skills: "I will never have good food again!" I laughed and cried at the same time.

<u>July 13, 2015</u>

It's never too early to think about college.

I recently took my 7-year-old son to see my alma mater, Lander University in Greenwood, SC.

"This place is awesome," Malachi proclaimed. "Do the guys share (dorm) rooms with the girls?"

I dodged the question, and told him I thought the school still has a theater program to accommodate his outrageousness.

<u>August 28, 2011</u>

Malachi found a photo of the Lander University Old Main tower.

"That's where I went to school," I told him proudly. He responded, "You went to school in a castle!" (It was more like a dungeon in the 1980s but has been refurbished.)

"Can I go to school in a castle?" he continued. "I want to be an astronaut."

I replied, "Study hard; maybe you can go to a castle for free. I hear there is a shortage of Ethiopian astronauts."

Malachi's dream comes at my expense. "I want to be on Disney (Channel)," my 7-year-old son has said repeatedly since our visit to Disney World earlier this summer. "Dad, when you get too old to do the news, you can come with me."

Perplexed by his comment, I asked, "How old is too old for me to do the news?" Malachi quickly replied, "48." At least I have a year to prepare for the move to L.A.

MISCOMMUNICATION

Malachi shouted with excitement for me to see his artwork on the bathroom mirror. "It's a masterpiece," my 6-year-old son declared of his purple marker on glass. "I'm Costco!"

"It's Picasso!" I replied probably too harshly, searching to find elements of cubism. If only Malachi could sell his work at Costco.

August 17, 2015

"Keep your hands in the tram at all times," said the driver of a parking shuttle at a nearby amusement park.

"What's a tramp?" 7-year-old Malachi asked loudly during the ride.
"It's a tram!" I scolded. "It's this train-like thing on wheels we are in."

Malachi replied, "I know that! What is a tramp?"

I started to say, "Do you see that woman three seats up?" Instead, I just said it's a woman who isn't well behaved.

February 24, 2015

Lego sets falling apart despite his best efforts left my 7-year-old son in pieces.

"I'm going to blow a casket," Malachi grumbled.
"Really," I replied. "Let me know who comes out of it."

Malachi tilted his head, calmed down, and asked, "What do you mean?"

"It's a gasket, not a casket!" I replied.
"Now, I'm really mad!" said the grumpy builder stomping away.

<u>May 12, 2014</u>

Malachi watched a video to learn about the eyes, ears, nose and throat.

"Look!" my 6-year-old son exclaimed. "It's the sarcophagus!"

"It's esophagus," I fired back, trying not to choke from laughter and require the coffin itself.

<u>September 17, 2011</u>

I spent much of the early morning restoring my Facebook account which was hacked.

Contrary to what was indicated this morning, I have not accepted a 23-year-old blonde and a 29-year-old brunette as "additional wives."

In addition, my professional credentials changed to "minister."

That may not be totally false since I can be ordained online in only 24 hours for as little as $68.

Go in peace.

March 14, 2012

I'm trying to help my 4-year-old son, Malachi, better understand our lives and surroundings. So, I gave him a quiz last night and soon realized I was "out of luck."

Jay: "Malachi, where do you live?"
Malachi: "Hendersonville."
Jay: "Where does Daddy work?"
Malachi: "...at the TV station."
Jay: "What's the name of it?"
Malachi: "W-S-O-L."

September 26, 2011

A long weekend with Malachi made me realize how difficult it might be for others to understand his terminology when Kelly and I aren't available.

So, I'm considering putting together a reference book for teachers, grandparents and friends.

Here are some of my favorites:
Washing McCleaner - Washing Machine
Kitchen Washing McCleaner - Dishwasher
Paper's Doctor - Veterinarian
Paper - Our cat, Caper
Lady Gaga - the pop star herself, or any woman who wears a large hat

TRAVELING

A motorist in front of Malachi and me weaved repeatedly.
I couldn't help noticing her bumper sticker: "Ain't Nothin' Better than Jesus."
"I'm glad she's a Christian," I told my 7-year-old son. "But, I don't think Jesus is happy with her driving." Malachi replied, "She drives like the devil."

September 8, 2015

Driving in Knoxville proved eventful. "Look, Dad, it's the Great Pyramid!" my 7-year-old son, Malachi, said of the triangular building along the Tennessee River. "That's the Marriott," I replied.

May 26, 2012

Driving along Airport Road yesterday, I became concerned when Malachi rolled down the window. "Hey man!" he yelled to the driver in the car next to us. "It's not Christmastime!"

Surprised by Malachi's outburst, I responded, "What is your problem?" Malachi replied, "See Daddy, there's a Christmas tree hanging in his car." It was an air freshener on the mirror.

September 15, 2011

A young woman with pigtails pulled out in front of me on Sweeten Creek Road. I hit the brakes and the horn simultaneously.

Pippi Longstocking didn't take kindly to that and gave me the one-finger salute from her sticker-covered, peace mobile.

Really agitated, I quipped, "You moron."

Malachi, in the backseat, asked, "Daddy, she's a moron?"

"Yes," I responded. "She needs to be more careful driving." (I need to be careful what I say.) Peace out.

September 28, 2011

The car alarm went off as I drove a station vehicle on I-40 yesterday.

Passing motorists began staring, pointing and laughing at me. I arrived at my destination making more noise than a fire engine.

On the way back to the station, the alarm again sounded. One driver in the opposite lane of Sweeten Creek Road pulled over, fearing I was an emergency vehicle or thief.

Now, the car has stopped wailing, but I haven't.

October 28, 2014

While traveling home through Columbia, SC, Malachi remarked, "This is paradise!"
Completely dumbfounded, I laughed and shook my head.
"This is Columbia!" I responded. "I once had a TV job here that lasted only two days. It's NOT paradise."

August 7, 2013

My ride home on I-26 was extraordinary yesterday! While driving from Asheville to Hendersonville, a young woman in a compact car began slowly passing me. I noticed she was changing clothes -- from a swimsuit to a server's uniform -- while, somehow, keeping her vehicle in its proper lane. I, on the other hand, weaved into the emergency lane.
I immediately realized I must slow down and allow her to pass completely. There was no need for me to wreck and be the bigger boob.

February 16, 2015

There were only two cars on I-26 westbound through Henderson County at 3:20 this morning: mine and the one riding my bumper for no reason. I need the sticker a man at church has on his car. It reads, "Do you follow God this close?"

CHURCH CHAT

The children's message on Pentecost Sunday, the birth of the church, was nearly the death of my career.

The minister compared the Holy Spirit to the wind, something you feel but can't see. She went on to describe the wind as part of a storm the prior night.

My 6-year-old son piped up, "My dad gets it wrong," to the laughter of the congregation. When Malachi returned to the pew, he gave me a high five and said, "Gotcha."

That he did.

May 13, 2015

A friend at church reminded me that Jeff Daniels of Dumb and Dumber fame will soon perform in Asheville.

"I want to go," Malachi said. "I've seen Dumb and Dumber."

I shook my head walking into the sanctuary and said, "Thanks for again making me look like parent of the year."

My 4-year-old son wants to be an acolyte at church, but I'm certain he's not ready to bring the flame in the sanctuary or extinguish it.

"I will say, 'Holy Spirit, FIRE, FIRE,'" Malachi told me in a loud cartoon voice.

I simply replied: "No, you won't, Beavis."

June 17, 2013

"Malachi, you look sharp," I said to my 5-year-old son on the way to church Sunday.
"I'm hot," he replied. "Strike a match!"
Humbleness has always been his strong point.

October 13, 2014

During mass on Sunday, Malachi chose to recite the priest's words in unison rather than the parishioners' response leading to communion.

"What are you doing?" I asked.

"Isn't it cool that I know it?" Malachi whispered.

"You're NOT the priest," I replied.

March 16, 2015

Malachi's greeting the priest after mass yesterday led to my downfall.

"He needs to be forgiven," Malachi told Father Praveen Boyapati, pointing to me.

I'm not sure which sin Malachi was referencing, but the priest laughed.

Malachi's pointing out someone's flaws is truly "the pot calling the kettle."

31

October 20, 2014

"Malachi, passing the peace of Christ does NOT mean giving the 'peace out' sign to people seated around you," I told my 6-year-old son.

December 2, 2014

Moments in church when you can talk only softly sometimes become awkward and hilarious. During a special music presentation Sunday, my match-making son struck again.

"Dad, is she married?" Malachi asked of the woman singing. "Yes!" I fired back loudly. "That's the music minister's wife."

"I don't see a ring," Malachi replied.
"There's a ring!" I answered. "Quit trolling for me."

September 9, 2013

"Daddy, why are you not going to sit with us in church?" my 5-year-old son asked Sunday morning.

"I have to read scripture (during the service)," I explained. "I will be sitting next to the minister." Malachi thought and then questioned: "So, you're going to be the pretend priest?"

That's so true in so many ways.

Why is it kids never hear what you want them to hear? Yet, they always hear what you don't want them to hear.

While waiting to play mini-golf while on vacation, Malachi grabbed the back of my pants. "What are you doing?" I asked in a harsh tone.

My 5-year-old son replied: "I'm kissing your butt." Outraged, I questioned, "Are you crazy? Why would you do that?"

Malachi answered matter-of-factly, "I'm just doing what you said that lady at church does to the new preacher."

September 1, 2014

"Ten dollars!" Malachi said to the usher... as my child placed his offering in the basket at church.
"Dude," I whispered, "you don't need to say anything about the amount!"
"Why?" my wide-eyed son asked.
"This is church, not a casino," I replied. "The amount is between you and God."

June 5, 2012

During the graduation breakfast at church on Sunday, Malachi ordered Coke to drink. I flinched. Fortunately, there wasn't any. First, my child didn't need Coke for breakfast. Secondly, I was afraid he was going to repeat what he said at dinner the other night, "Yes, I like Coke; my daddy likes Coke with medicine in it."

MISBEHAVING

Malachi opened an umbrella on the porch and subsequently punched out the glass on the front door.

"I've seen people use trash bags in place of a car window, but never for the front door," I said to my destructive 6-year-old son. "This falls under the category: 'You might be a Redneck if...'"

June 22, 2014

I warned Malachi the other night to be polite at dinner.

Unfortunately, my 6-year-old son didn't equate that with being tactful.

The restaurant manager stopped at our table and asked if everything was okay.

"I had the hamburger. I liked it; it was good," my son said without prompting and to my liking. Then, Malachi continued: "But, when I was four, I came here and got the crab legs and threw up."

August 31, 2013

We just returned from a wedding ceremony in Mills
River where two of our older, widowed friends
exchanged vows. Before the reception, Malachi asked
the bride: "Are you going to have a baby?" She laughed,
but could just as easily have asked me: "Are you going
to control your child?"

July 8, 2013

"Why would you open your window in the car wash?" I
asked in disgust and amazement.
"I was hot," Malachi answered casually, as water and
soap filled the cabin of the car.
"Now, I'm hot!" I grimaced to my 5-year-old son.
He replied, "Then turn on the air."

January 21, 2012

I leaned over at the dinner table last night to help
Malachi with his meal.

"It's a circle," he said, pointing to my bald spot. "Why's
it there?"
"Old age," I replied.
"Will more hair fall out?" Malachi continued.
My response: "Most definitely with your antics."

February 4, 2015

I realized yesterday little has changed for Malachi and me since my son turned 7. We both still lack tact.
My child repeated at school "that Daddy said the teacher was driving him to the end of the Earth" because of the large volume of homework.
That probably didn't go over well.
Instead of Legos, could someone have given Malachi the gift of discretion for his birthday?

August 11, 2014

Malachi has said for a couple of years he wants to be a Catholic priest when he grows up. His actions, however, have me questioning his career choice. Here's why:

1. Priests are not materialistic.
"Daddy, you said I could get a surprise at Target if I was good at the party," Malachi reminded, following a recent event.
"Yes, I did," I replied. "Can I get two?" Malachi pleaded.

2. Priests shun romance.
Malachi learned a classmate is not returning to his school this fall. "I'm sad," my 6-year-old son exclaimed. "She has the best cheeks for kissing."

3. Priests are forgiving and not judgmental.
"Malachi, telling your grandmother during a disagreement she 'has the devil in her heart' was inappropriate," I scolded. "Apologize and mean it!"

March 5, 2015

I didn't know whether to yell, spank, or high five after Malachi's latest prank.

While I slept, he took all the toothpaste from the bathroom, removed the tops, and lined the tubes at my bedroom doorway. You can imagine the mess I made stepping on various Crest gels and pastes in the wee hours.

I got the last laugh by making the 7-year-old prankster clean it up.

April 14, 2014

Malachi performed a magic show for the family last night. The 6-year-old magician's words went something like this: "Abracadabra, abrakazoo, make my dad turn to poo." It was a quick show lacking applause.

July 6, 2011

An idle threat I made to my son came back to haunt me at the Pirates' House restaurant in Savannah this past weekend. I recently told Malachi if he didn't quit spitting I was going to put hot pepper in his mouth. (I would never do this, but he apparently doesn't realize that.) Malachi saw a baby at the next table spit up. My child yelled, "Daddy, get the hot pepper; he's spitting!" Check please.

February 17, 2014

I heard Malachi in the dining room over the weekend saying: "I win... I lose... I win."

"What are you doing?" I asked my 6-year-old son as I approached from the hallway.
"I'm opening cards," he said of his Valentine's mail. "If they have money in them, I say 'win.' If they don't have money, I say 'lose.'"

Trying to hold back laughter, I lectured him on the importance of being grateful people remembered him at all -- cash or not. This child is COSTING me my sanity.

April 9, 2012

I hope Malachi becomes a defense attorney because he's the best at deflecting the issue at hand and creating confusion.

Here's what happened Saturday night.

Jay: "Malachi, it's time for your bath."
Malachi: "No."
Jay: "You're stinky; go get in the bathtub."
Malachi: "No, Daddy, you stink!"
Jay: "Quit being a smart butt, and get in that bathroom!"
Malachi: "Ahhhhh... Mommy, Daddy said a bad word! He said butt! I can't believe it. Daddy said a bad word!"

February 18, 2013

"Malachi, shouting 'fire the cannon' while using the bathroom is not appropriate, especially at someone else's house," I said in disbelief Saturday night.

June 3, 2013

"Don't refer to me as 'Your Majesty,'" I scolded Malachi. "Got it?"
"Yes, SIRE," he replied. "Got it."

February 14, 2012

I'm on the brink of insanity because my words are being taken too literally by my son, Malachi. During dinner, he began drumming on his plate.

"Dude," I said, "knock it off!" So, he did -- right in the floor.

I told Malachi I was quickly losing patience. His response: "Where did they go?" Arrrrrgggggghhhhh!

June 8, 2012

Here is a piece of advice I felt the need to give Malachi before visiting a Catholic school on Thursday.
"Please be respectful," I said. "If you see a nun, don't refer to her as 'the lady in a penguin suit.'"

April 13, 2012

Driving little Johnnie Cochran through the Drive-Thru at Chick-fil-A yesterday seemed like a good idea until he learned cheesecake and lemon pie are no longer on the menu.

"What?" Malachi yelled into the speaker. "That's not right! Why don't you have cheesecake?"

The inquiry evolved into badgering the attendant at the pick-up window. Malachi didn't accept her explanation that new desserts are coming.

"That's mean," he argued of the absence of the triangular slices. The only thing missing was the comment: "If you don't have pie, then I must cry."

November 2, 2013

Malachi came home from school with the previous day's homework assignment marked with X's.

"What the heck is this?" I asked, realizing the instructions hadn't been followed.

"Mimi helped me with it," Malachi said, referring to my mother. ("Some help she was," I quipped in disgust.)

"Don't be mad," my 5-year-old son pleaded. "She's an old lady."

October 30, 2012

I must teach my child better bathroom etiquette, especially before we go to another upscale place. Dressed as a pirate for a Halloween party, Malachi began questioning the man in the adjacent restroom stall at the Grove Park Inn on Saturday.

"Hi, in there," my child squeaked.
"Hi," a nervous man mumbled.
"Whatcha doin' in there?"

At this point, I told Malachi to quit talking, take care of business, and then wash his hands. The attendant was laughing; I was mortified.

Malachi ran out of the restroom telling everyone in the hallway: "The toilet flushed itself!"

May 17, 2013

Malachi has good reason to call me a "soda jerk." I made him a milkshake the other night while half asleep. "It's yucky!" my 5-year-old son shouted in disgust after one sip. "It's the worst milkshake ever!"

It turns out in haste I mixed chocolate syrup and ice cream with buttermilk rather than regular milk. "It was an accident," I said apologetically.

"No it wasn't," Malachi replied. "It was a trick!"
Whatever the case, it was funny.

August 15, 2011

There is nothing like the smell of honeysuckle!
Malachi locked himself in the bathroom over the
weekend and sprayed a half-bottle of air freshener on the
sink, toilet and himself.

"It smells good," he said, exiting the bathroom stronger
than a flower garden in early bloom.

I retorted, "You smell like an old lady!" Two showers
later, bees no longer follow him.

March 18, 2012

My child entered the bathroom at our house this morning
and became distraught.

Malachi: "Daddy, the carpet is gone!"
Jay: "It's a rug, and it's being washed."
Malachi: "Where is it?"
Jay: "I left it outside to dry... and now it's really wet."
Malachi: "You left it outside in the rain?"
Jay: "I did."
Malachi: "That was dumb."
Jay: "Thanks."

February 26, 2012

Malachi went to my parents' house for the weekend, but it wasn't long before I got the call.

"Daddy, I want to come home," he said in a pitiful voice. "Why?" I asked. He responded only "because I want to."

That meant he was in trouble for bad behavior, though my parents were too polite to admit that. I did not pick him up early, but on the way home my suspicions about Malachi's actions were confirmed. "Daddy," he said, "Papa yells like you do." I remember well.

September 21, 2011

The telephone rang last night, and I picked up the phone upstairs to discover it had been disconnected from the wall... probably by a 3-year-old.

The incident reminded me of a story my grandfather told about a struggling Spartanburg lawyer.
The attorney saw a man coming in to the office, so he picked up the phone and began talking... using impressive legal terminology. Sounding important, the lawyer asked "the caller" to hold while he acknowledged the visitor.

"Yes sir, what can I do for you?" the lawyer asked.
The bewildered man replied: "I'm here to hook up your phone."

MAKEUP

The other day at dinner we saw a woman powdering her face with a Clinique compact.

Malachi yelled: "Look Daddy, that's (like) yours."

I didn't know whether to laugh or cry.

Either way, MAKEUP!

May 13, 2013

It seemed like a good idea at the time to take Malachi with me while buying my makeup for TV.

I asked the Clinique consultant if she had any concealer for Malachi to cover up a blemish before his school pictures this week.

My son grew increasingly leery of his surroundings, spying "the long Q-tips." "I don't want her to use those in my ears," he said, now noticing the cotton balls in a glass jar. "Am I going to get a shot?"

I tried to reassure Malachi this was not the doctor's office. "Yes it is," he replied. "That's a doctor in the store!" Visits to the makeup counter are always traumatic for guys.

July 22, 2015

My 7-year-old son heard me comment the other night I was running out of makeup for work. A few days later our conversation went something like this:

Malachi: "Dad, did you get your makeup?"
Jay: "Not yet."
Malachi: "Why not?"
Jay: "I haven't had time."
Malachi: "You need to get your makeup so you won't look like a scary ghost on TV."

February 1, 2012

Malachi overheard me talking about redecorating, and that spurred his creativity in the downstairs bathroom.

He smeared red makeup, white hair gel and blue toothpaste on the toilet bowl, lid and tank.

"Why did you do this?" I asked.

"Because it's beautiful," Malachi confidently replied of his patriotic artwork. I realize art is in the eye of the beholder, but my child is no Jasper Johns!

December 3, 2011

I knew it was only a matter of time before the "his" and "hers" makeup drawers caused problems.

Malachi came out of the bathroom wearing Kelly's blush and my Clinique powder. I told him boys don't wear makeup!

He responded, "But, you do Daddy."

Frustrated, I responded, "Only for work, now get that off!"

I don't have time to deal with little RuPaul.

SPORTS

I am more convinced than ever as a coach that Little League sports are out of control.

Granted, I've had my share of disputes with umpires and opposing coaches over the years, but last night was a first for me. A grandparent of one of my players threatened to deck me because his grandson continuously plays the same position.

I'll be back on the field tomorrow, wearing the extra set of catcher's gear while brushing up on my Tae Kwon Do.

March 23, 2015

I must not be doing a good job as a baseball coach explaining positions. "Who's going to be the bench waiter?" Malachi asked.

"That's bench warmer!" I replied after a long pause. "We have several candidates."

Still insisting it is "bench waiter," Malachi continued, "That's the person who gets to bring everybody else Gatorade."

I now have a frontrunner for the job!

"Go Mets!" Those are two words I thought I'd never say. But Malachi's T-ball team is the Mets. He is enthusiastic about batting and scoring, but I wish he'd stop climbing the centerfield fence and pay more attention on defense. Still, I realized how serious he is about baseball when he said the blessing before dinner last night. It ended, "...give us Lord our daily bread. Amen. Go Mets!"

<u>May 7, 2012</u>

It's a situation I'm trying to slide away from.

Malachi hit the ball toward third base, but made a head-first slide into first base during Saturday's T-Ball game. His batting helmet came off, and he was covered in dirt and chalk.

"Why did you slide into first?" I asked, perplexed because the ball was never thrown near first base.

"Because, I saw it on TV," Malachi replied, getting high fives.

On the way home, I wanted to tell him, "You can't do something just because you see it on TV!"

Then, I realized I might be putting myself out of business, so I just said, "Good play; that would have made the highlight reel."

<u>April 29, 2015</u>

Called in to play catcher the other night during a Little League game, a coach asked Malachi if he wore his "cup."
"No, I don't like it," my 7-year-old son replied. "It hurts. The cup is not big enough."
"That's what all guys say!" I replied. "Remember to wear it."

"Daddy, are you going to be the vampire?" my soon-to-be 5-year-old asked.
"What are you talking about?" I inquired, violating my own rule against answering a question with a question.
"I'm talking about my baseball games," Malachi responded. "Are you going to be the vampire?"
"It's UMPIRE," I explained. "No, I will not be umpiring.'
(There's no reason to give people more reason to dislike me.)

April 3, 2012

I've made the baseball umpire the bad guy in my quest to get Malachi to behave on the diamond during T-ball games.

"If you start acting ridiculous and running around, he will throw you out," I said to Malachi of the umpire "He's in charge of the game."

Malachi thought for a second and responded, "Why's he gonna pick me up and throw me over the fence?"

(That may be the only way to get him out of the park and get the point across.)

April 14, 2015

I took a beating yesterday on my last day of vacation.

First, I went to the dermatologist and had a spot removed from my face. Hours later, I got hit in the forehead with a foul ball at Malachi's baseball game.

"What do I look like?" I asked while getting into my car after the game.

"A nitwit," my 7-year-old son replied.

September 30, 2013

An afternoon run with my 5-year-old son nearly turned deadly, according to him.

We were near the end of our journey when Malachi noticed angry yellow jackets swarming from the ground at the edge of the path. "Run," Malachi yelled, grabbing my hand for the next quarter mile. "I saved your life, Daddy."

Grateful and perplexed I asked, "Don't you think you are taking this a little too far?"

Malachi replied with a question, "Did you have your medicine (EpiPen)?" I responded, "no."
"Then, I saved your life," my son said with certainty.
Point taken.

MEDICAL

Getting a flu shot was never more painful.

Malachi and I went to a local pharmacy where a beautiful, young, blonde physician assistant prepared to administer our vaccines.

"Are you married?" my 6-year-old son asked her.
"No, I'm not," she replied.

"Good," Malachi continued. "My first (birth) mom died; my second (adopted) mom died; I need a new mom, and my dad needs a new wife."

"Hey chief," I said to Malachi. "Thanks for making me out to be a serial killer."

April 22, 2015

It's ironic that on Monday 4/20, the day to unofficially celebrate cannabis culture, I received a reminder for Malachi and me to soon come to the dentist.

"Will I see the 'high dentist?'" my 7-year-old son asked.

"It's hygienist!" I replied laughing, offering no explanation of his innocent drug humor.

June 18, 2014

Malachi informed me when I came home the other day he had cancelled my annual doctor's appointment for a physical exam.

"The phone rang. A lady said 'press 3 to cancel,' so I did," my 6-year-old son explained.

"Why would you cancel it?" I asked in disgust. "You're hyperactive, and I need medication!"

Smiling, while running to the other room, Malachi replied, "Maybe you should go to the doctor!"

November 8, 2012

Milking the pain of vaccinations for all they were worth, Malachi told me, "The doctor said I can't get a bath."

"Really," I replied skeptically. "What did the doctor say about going to bed early?"

"He said I should stay up ALL night."

I asked a second question, as my child grabbed my soda can, "What did the doctor say about drinking Coke?"

Malachi answered confidently, "He said it was ok."

"You're ok," I said, ending the conversation. "Quit manipulating me!"

May 24, 2011

I thought spilling Coke in the car, or coffee on a white shirt was bad until yesterday. I realized it could be MUCH worse. At the doctor's office, I saw a woman slosh her liquid specimen. I retreated to the other bathroom to laugh. "You're in luck" just didn't hold.

September 17, 2012

I'm working on a story for 5 p.m. about a really cool website that uses a personality test to match patients with compatible doctors. I just took the test, only to learn my best match is a gynecologist. Since I know her, I'm going to call and make my appointment.

September 13, 2011

I took Malachi to the doctor yesterday. In the waiting area, he began showing the nurse what was wrong with his knee.

This reminded me of a health story I covered a few years ago regarding a hip replacement. The elderly patient pulled down her pants in the waiting area to "show me her scar." I remain scarred for life.

ENCOUNTERS

I picked up my 4-year-old child from school to find he had rolled his jeans up to his ankles and buttoned the top button on a knit shirt. "You look like a dork!" I said to Malachi without thinking.
"What's a dork?" he asked.
"It's like a goofball," I responded, still lacking tact.
"That's not good," Malachi replied with wide eyes, now rolling down the jeans and reaching for his neckline.
"You look better," I complimented. "You were only one pair of glasses and suspenders away from being Urkel."

July 16, 2013

Microphones are important and troublesome in TV. Over the years, I've sat on them, left them "on" while taking a bathroom break, and, too often, failed to turn them "on."

I felt better, though, after hearing a minister's sermon on Sunday. She told the story of a priest preparing to deliver his first sermon.

The congregation had been told to embrace his first words with an enthusiastic "...and also with you."

After entering the sanctuary, he began tapping the microphone and muttered, "There's something wrong with this microphone."

The congregation dutifully responded, "...and also with you!"

September 8, 2015

The Apple Festival came with the biggest surprise.

"It's so nice to meet you, Mr. Cessarich," a woman said to me.
"You're funny," I replied.
"John, you know weather," she continued, truly mistaking me for the WYFF meteorologist.
"You don't know me," I thought to myself.

<u>June 22, 2015</u>

When I woke up yesterday morning, I shouted, "It's Father's Day!"

Malachi ran to me and said he had made me "a money tree."

Covering his mouth, my 7-year-old son mumbled, "It was supposed to be a surprise." With wilted leaves and paper-clipped dollar bills, it was still a surprise.

Priceless.

January 12, 2015

I pulled up to the drive-thru window to pay for my meal last week.
"Are you the news guy?" the teenager taking my money asked.
"Yes, I am," I replied. "Thank you for watching."
She continued questioning, "Are you Bob Caldwell?"
"No," I replied sheepishly. "I'm not Bob. I'm Jay."
Malachi from the backseat chirped, "She thought you were the car guy. That's funny."
Hilarious.

September 15, 2014

I'm preparing to mark a major milestone: 20 years since my most embarrassing moment on TV. I was working at WJHL-TV in Johnson City, TN, covering a story about strippers arrested for indecent exposure. When I interviewed one of the "dancers" on live TV, she proved she had been well coached to turn the tables. She put her hand on my shoulder and said, "Oh, Jay, it's so good to see you again."

August 1, 2014

While standing in the receiving line during one of the visitations following Kelly's death, an elderly lady approached and grasped my hand. "I just want you to know how sorry I am," she said softly. "When the time is right, I want you to meet my daughter."

August 1, 2014

I took Malachi to a doctor's office in South Carolina to establish him as a patient in case he needed medical care while visiting his grandparents. The receptionist immediately asked me regarding my son: "You gotcha custody papers?" Apparently, in her world, a white man can't be the father of a black child without documents from DSS, law enforcement, or the court system.

April 21, 2014

Shopping on the day before Easter proved no better than Christmas Eve. First, the crowds slowed me; then a sales clerk annoyed me. While checking out at one store, the young associate said, "I know you from somewhere!" I made the mistake of responding, "...perhaps from TV?"

"No, that's not it," she immediately replied. "I go to Brevard College and my dad went to Brevard College and you look like one of HIS old professors."

March 26, 2014

My colleagues are amused by a thank you note I received this morning from a second grader. I recently visited her school for a weather presentation. Her message includes the question, "Is it hard being a forecaster?" She implies I'm not always accurate, and her artwork includes an eerie smile. "Do you have any friends?" she closes with in pencil on construction paper. I must have made quite the impression.

February 3, 2014

Malachi informed me he doesn't believe one of the girls in his class at school will be attending his birthday party. "Why do you think that?" I asked my now 6-year-old son.

"Because I kissed her on the lips," he replied.
"Why did you do that?" I asked with a raised voice, eyebrow and forehead.

"It's your fault," Malachi replied. "You said I could only kiss my girlfriend on the lips."
Perhaps I should have continued, "I don't mean now."

February 28, 2014

A viewer called the station after I anchored my first newscast in Tennessee more than 20 years ago. "You remind me of a movie star," she said. I thanked her. She quickly responded, "It's not a compliment; you look and sound like Gilbert Gottfried!"

December 9, 2013

Leaving the U.S. Cellular Center after Sesame Street Live, a man asked: "What's the weather?"
I politely gave him the forecast.
Malachi later asked, while walking down the window-filled corridor at the arena, "Why couldn't he just look out the window?"
I thought to myself, "I like your way of thinking."

November 19, 2013

The phone call I recently received at my desk ranks No. 2 on my all-time favorite list.

A foul-mouthed woman told me that her husband's former wife had mailed her literally "a box of crap" via UPS. Somehow, the caller thought this was a health story, yet refused to give her name or phone number.

Before she abruptly hung up, I thought to myself, "See what brown can do for you."

I'll save my No. 1 favorite call for another time.

January 13, 2013

An afternoon run for Malachi and me probably has one woman believing I'm the evil park patrol.

Malachi began slowing down on the final lap of our two-mile journey, and I yelled: "Pick it up! Pick it up!"

Unfortunately, a nearby woman next to her squatting dog looked at me in horror and nervously responded, "I am. I am."

I explained to the woman I was referring to my son's pace and not her dog's droppings. I don't think she believed me.

I've become accustomed over the years to being mistaken for my colleague Sherrill Barber.

It's happened at church, the hospital, and restaurants, but the latest case of mistaken identity is my favorite.

I was pumping gas in Mills River when a man yelled, "Sherrill Barber!"

Before I could correct him, he began critiquing News 13 personalities.

"I just love you, Sherrill," he said with a raspy Southern drawl fast enough, though, to prevent me from getting in a word.

"I like Larry and Darcel," he continued matter-of-factly.

"I like 'em girls in the mornin', Julie and Holly, but that Jay Siltzer is a smart @$s, and I don't care much for him."

I thanked the man for watching, but never told him my real name.

I didn't want to ruin a good Facebook post.

April 22, 2013

There was almost one less person at the family reunion Saturday.

Malachi and I swung by my parents' house to give them a ride to the event. Dad began taking food through the garage to load into my car when Mom pressed the button to close the garage door, nearly pinning the family patriarch.

"Gee whiz!" my father exclaimed. "What are you trying to do to me?"

Malachi chimed in: "Mimi, you almost cut Papa in two."

My mother apologized and said she was grateful my dad escaped harm and didn't require hospitalization.

"Hospital, nothing!" Dad fired back. "I would have been at Shepherd's (funeral home) with deviled eggs in one hand and cupcakes in the other."

February 11, 2012

Skirting the truth got me in trouble while driving Malachi home from daycare. We drove past the liquor store on Sweeten Creek Road -- the one with the big, neon green abc letters. "What's that?" Malachi asked. "Ughhh," I paused. "It's the letter store." I kept driving, as my son began screaming, "I want to go in and see the letter store!" Suddenly, I had the same thought.

March 25, 2013

While washing our hands in a restroom in the Upstate over the weekend, a child walked in looking perplexed. "Are you his dad?" the youngster asked me, pointing to Malachi.

"Yes," I answered, "this is my son."
Having difficulty accepting this, the child said to me "...but, but, you're supposed to be black."

"Not necessarily," I fired back quickly. "Families can come in all colors. God has adopted us all and loves us the same."

Maybe this spurred a discussion for the child at home, or perhaps he was further confused.

January 18, 2013

My 4-year-old son saw on TV last night that a man using a metal detector along the coast of Australia found a giant gold nugget worth up to $500,000. "I want to go to the beach in Savannah and find gold," Malachi said. Kelly, already planning Malachi's upcoming birthday, added, "Oh, I know, let's get him a metal detector!" I'm curious; does Fisher-Price make one? It could provide hours of entertainment for Malachi while potentially paying for the vacation, his education, and a new home.

December 27, 2012

On the first day after Christmas, my 4-year-old said to me, "I know what I want for my birthday!"

Malachi doesn't turn 5 for more than a month, but told me he wants a Chick-fil-A party for his friends. Gasping for air because of his timing, I asked him if he'd consider his friends bringing goods for a food bank instead of gifts for him.

"I'll do it if the priest can see them," he responded after careful thought, clearly trying to score points.

Can someone please give my child discretion and humbleness for his birthday?

November 27, 2012

I went to Malachi's school the other day, and a woman approached, saying she enjoyed seeing me on TV.

Somewhat flattered, I told her, "Thank you for watching!"

Unfortunately, she continued, "Larry Blunt, I didn't know you had a grandchild here."

For once, I was speechless.

October 6, 2012

Malachi may be a journalist yet. After seeing two jugglers toss knives around me on the morning show Friday, my 4-year-old son asked the right questions.

Malachi: "Daddy, why did those men throw knives at you?"
Jay: "They are professional jugglers and weren't trying to hit me."
Malachi: "Can I throw knives at you?"
Jay: "You already do."

July 2, 2012

Never wear a red polo and khakis into Target.

I made that mistake the other day and was mistaken for a store employee repeatedly. The first two times I was nice to customers with questions and explained: "I'm sorry; I don't work here."

The third time, however, I sent a man to "aisle 14" in his quest for laundry products. (Plus, I thanked him for shopping at Target.)

I don't know if there is an aisle 14, but it sounded good. This experience has me reconsidering wearing my blue vest to Lowe's or my orange apron to Home Depot.

Malachi has been telling me about the "new girl" in his class that's cute. I saw her this morning and she is adorable, though a head taller than my son.

"Is that your girlfriend?" I asked Malachi, who responded by nodding and blushing.

"You guys kinda have the Sonny and Cher thing going on," I added.

Malachi, looking perplexed, asked: "Who are they?" I told him they were popular singers when I was his age.

"Can we listen to them?" he asked. I didn't respond because the last thing I want him saying to his new friend is: "I Got You Babe."

May 14, 2012

I ran into one of the children's leaders from our church while Mother's Day shopping with my son on Saturday. I apologized to her that Malachi had missed choir practice the previous Wednesday.

"I had an accident," Malachi interjected, offering far more information than I had planned. "I had to go home; I peed on myself."

After that response, I almost did the same.

June 17, 2012

A quick dinner last night with the family almost made me sick.

It had nothing to do with the food; my hamburger was great. The problem centered on the woman seated across from me with her backside exposed. She needed high-waist jeans or, at least, a courtesy thong.

Each time I made eye contact with Kelly or Malachi, all I saw was a large posterior. (If she'd looked anything like Beyonce or J. Lo., I'd probably still be at Hot Dog World.)

I made no mention of the incident at the time, but I find I can no longer hold it in -- kind of like the woman herself.

April 10, 2012

More than two hours in the morning is a long time to be on the set without a bathroom break. Usually, I have to make a pit stop, but I learned years ago the importance of turning off the microphone in the restroom.

Some 15 years ago, I was filling in as the news anchor at WJHL-TV in Johnson City, and nature called. The person on audio didn't kill my mic, and the toilet flush went out over air. It happened just as the meteorologist was giving his hurricane forecast. He laughed; I could have died; that whole show went down the toilet.

March 29, 2012

I am thrilled there will be a sequel to Anchorman. If the producers need material for the bungling news reader, I can provide options from personal experience.

Once on the radio, I pronounced Penelope... Pin-uh-LOPE.

A couple of years ago on the morning show, I called a suspect Jesus, rather than Hay-zeus.
Still, it's not as bad as a former colleague who, while anchoring with me, referred to an I.E.D. (in Iraq) as an I.U.D.

To quote Ron Burgundy: "It is what I say it is."

March 28, 2012

I had always wondered if any women actually wear those tiny, thong bikinis featured in the annual Sports Illustrated issue. The answer is yes.

On Tybee Island, GA, last week, Malachi spotted a 20-something-year-old hottie sporting only spandex in strategic areas.

"What's she wearing, Daddy?" Malachi asked.

"It's her swimsuit," I replied. "She packed light."

March 13, 2012

I overheard a couple of my colleagues talking about their days as candy stripers at local hospitals.

The conversation brought back memories of the time in 1990 I wrote a story for The Index-Journal about an award-winning candy striper in Greenwood, SC. There was one problem: I misspelled striper and repeatedly referred to her in print as a candy STRIPPER.

Her father was furious and stormed into the newspaper, demanding a retraction because his teen-angel had been implied to be a pole-dancing floozie. I convinced him a correction would just draw more attention to the situation.

March 7, 2012

This month is the 20th anniversary of "Shoe Time" at the McCormick County Courthouse in South Carolina.

A defendant's mother in court wrapped the straps of her large purse around this reporter's ankle and pulled.

My Bass Weejun went flying toward the bench. "I'll see you in chambers," the judge said to me, holding my shoe and threatening a charge of contempt.

Fortunately, he believed my explanation, but I was forever known in McCormick as "Shoeless Jay."

February 22, 2012

"You look so much better in person," a woman told me yesterday while I was working on a health story in Hendersonville.

"What does that really mean?" I asked her. "Are you saying I look like crap on TV?"

Fortunately she laughed, and went on to explain I look taller, fatter and older on her TV.

How do I fix this? I'm 5'-7" and 150 pounds; I can't do much about that. Perhaps I should have visited the cosmetics counter at the mall to begin age-defying treatments.

February 19, 2012

I'm not a beer drinker, but almost no one around me this past weekend would believe that. Sitting near the bar at Applebee's last night, Malachi inquired about a neon crown with distinct lettering under it.

"It's a Budweiser sign," I explained. "It says 'King of Beers.'"

Case closed... until our trip to Ingles this afternoon. A man passed us on an aisle with a cart filled with Budweiser. Malachi yelled, "Hey man, that's the King of Beers!" I had just as soon the Clydesdales trampled me right then.

February 9, 2012

I read a story online this morning about a mule kicking a man. It reminded me of a funny story my grandfather told about our family.

Two men visited Uncle Horace, who was ailing. Afterward, the first man asked the other why Horace was so strange.

The second man replied: "...because he was kicked by a mule."

The first man quipped: "You wouldn't have thought it would have kicked the whole family."

January 13, 2012

I spoke yesterday to a group of nursing students at A-B Tech about my cancer experiences. There isn't much funny about cancer.

Still, I did tell them about my return to work in Knoxville in 1999 following my surgery and radiation treatments for testicular cancer.

 A co-worker at WVLT-TV left a card and Walmart (smiley face) rollback ball on my desk. The note simply said, "This is to replace the one that got away."

December 15, 2011

I feel especially bad for retail sales associates this time
of year. I spent years working at Belk during high school
and college and found out how rude customers can be.

Once a lady threw a shoe at me; another slapped me in
the face.

One holiday shopper complained my gift wrapping of a
stroller looked as if a child had done it. I told her no one
would guess what it was.

November 25, 2011

I think my son has been listening to too much Lady
Gaga.

Before I sent him and Kelly off to my in-laws for
Thanksgiving, I told Malachi to say please, thank you,
and yes ma'am or yes sir.

Disgusted with me for my repeated reminders, he
responded, "Daddy, you're putting me on the edge, the
edge, the edge..."

I now understand why Gaga calls her fans "Little
Monsters."

November 21, 2011

Sorority girls fawned over Malachi during dinner the other night at Applebee's.

He loved the attention from the young women, some of whom probably have fathers younger than I am. I began thinking that while in college 25 years ago I should have borrowed a small, cute child to get girls' attention. It does work; I had more 20-year-old women talk to me Friday night than I did during all the 1980s.

My "feeling young time," though, was short lived once one girl said "sir," and another asked if I was a grandfather.

November 20, 2011

It was one of those times it was inappropriate to laugh, but that didn't stop me.

Following a Thanksgiving lunch at church, a storyteller gathered the young children and told them their ancestors were likely on The Mayflower.

I chuckled to the person next to me, "I'm thinking not so much in Malachi's case. I have great doubt there were any Ethiopians there."

November 14, 2011

My child got in my dad's hair, literally, and the result wasn't good. Malachi flipped Dad's comb-over, told him he needed a haircut, and then said he was bald.

I told Malachi to be nicer to the main sponsor of his college fund.

After learning about this, I apologized to Dad and explained Malachi says "the first thing that comes to mind without thinking."

My father responded, "Wonder who he gets that from?"

July 13, 2011

Looking ahead to tomorrow, I see where it's National Nude Day.

No, I won't participate.

But, a previous station I worked for once had a reporter who frequently had her own "naked days."

Colleagues dropping by her apartment to pick up newsroom keys or camera gear discovered her vacuuming, cooking, or talking on the phone in the nude.

I never met her... so sad.

November 6, 2011

My wait to make a purchase at a department store turned into an episode of "Mama's Family." A woman behind me was on her phone to her elderly mother.

Woman on phone: "Mama, it's 7:25, and you've missed Wheel of Fortune."
Jay (thinking to himself): "The Wheel will spin again on Monday."
Woman on phone: "No, Mama, I won't go to the ABC store for you again today."
Jay (thinking again): "Now I need to go there."
Woman on phone: "Mama, I can't tell you what I want to say because the newsman is in front of me."

This is why I shop online.

October 31, 2011

Malachi watched his first episode of "The Addams Family" this past weekend. He liked the music, the pet lion Kitty Kat and The Thing.

"I want one," he said of the occasionally appearing hand.
"Me too," I replied.
"Where do we get one?" Malachi persisted. "I want Santa to bring me a helping hand!"
This could be a problem.

October 27, 2011

My thought for the day centers on "Trick or Treat," as presented to me by one of my college philosophy professors. If a child comes to my house, rings the doorbell and says "Trick or Treat?" then I'm correct to trick him.

The child said "Trick OR Treat?" so I have fulfilled my obligation by providing no treats and implementing the prank.

September 6, 2011

It wasn't my most embarrassing moment on TV this morning, but pretty close.

Traffic reporter George Sheldon tossed to the break, but Holly and I came back on.

She was crouched over the computer; I was vigorously brushing what little hair I have. It was awful!

Still, it wasn't as bad as the time in Knoxville I swallowed a bug during a live shot, or the time in Johnson City a stripper on camera said: "good to see you again."

September 2, 2011

Malachi's way of handling confrontation is personal. A taller child got in his face, demanding the toy he was holding.

Malachi told the youngster: "Your breath stinks. You need to brush your teeth!"

The child turned around and walked away.

When I learned about this, I didn't know whether to say, "Good job, son!" or "Wow, you're more obnoxious than I am."

<u>September 1, 2011</u>

A woman came up to me today and said, "I've seen you somewhere before."

Somewhat flattered, I responded: "...perhaps on Channel 13."

She snapped back, "No, that's not it. I think it was at the funeral home."

Sympathetically, I asked, "Were we there at the same time paying our respects?"

"No," she responded. "You sold me a casket."
I was left dead speechless.

<u>August 3, 2011</u>

I opened my mail and found a portfolio from a college student wanting me "to review" her modeling photos. She was under-dressed.

Why would she send this to me? Do I look like Hugh Hefner? I don't own a smoking jacket or a mansion.

The only bunnies at my house pertain to dust or Fisher-Price toys.

I mailed everything back to her. Please, keep your nude photos to yourself.

February 18, 2015

Malachi confessed he is in love with my co-worker,
Ingrid.

"When she comes on, I kiss the TV," my 7-year-old son
admitted.

"OK," I replied and then questioned. "What do you do
when Holly and I come on?"

"I wave," Malachi answered. "But Ingrid is so beautiful,
I have to kiss her!" Here's proof.

July 26, 2011

Splashville in Downtown Asheville left Malachi and me all wet in more ways than one after church on Sunday.

After an hour at the spray park, clouds built, and I told Malachi we had to leave because storms were coming.

He ran and told every child there to "get out... it's gonna storm."

Getting no response or reaction, he yelled, "My daddy's the weatherman!" Little man, welcome to my world of being ignored.

May 31, 2011

A lot of teenagers are beginning their first summer job, but I don't want to hear their complaints about how bad it is.

My first summer job was at the Fort Pulaski National Monument in Savannah when I was 15. I thought I was going to be a tour guide. The only things I toured were the bathrooms, cleaning them all summer.

Each time I pass by the park on the way to Tybee Island, I still refer to it as "Fort P-U."

May 18, 2011

A friend recently had her photo taken with President
Carter. I'm glad she had a better experience with him
than I did. More than 20 years ago I interviewed him in
Columbia. Before the meeting, I went to the men's room,
got locked in the stall and had to climb over it to get out.
As I made my leap, Mr. Carter walked in to the
restroom. No one said anything, but it sure made for an
awkward Q&A later.

May 4, 2011

Some people worry about black cats crossing their paths.
I'm concerned about skunks. This morning an entire
skunk family walked across the parking lot at WLOS as I
drove in to work. I did nothing. I learned my lesson last
year when I blew my horn at a skunk. He tooted back...
and the car detailing was expensive.

April 19, 2011

Brenda Anders was in the studio today, taping kitchen
and craft segments. I don't know how she can look at me
without laughing. A few years ago she made cookies and
I commented to co-anchor Bob Caldwell (now retired)
how dry and spicy they were. He quickly told me I had
eaten the dog biscuits she had made for Pet Pals.

March 21, 2011

A story this morning about a science olympiad took me down a path of destruction. I was forced to recount the model rocket I built years ago. It looked great! But, after launch, it caught fire and set the field ablaze next to the old T.L. Hanna High School in Anderson. It turns out I was concerned about the appearance of the rocket and didn't pay attention when packing the components.

July 7, 2014

The camera never lies, and never has that been more true than the other day.
While standing in line at a food court near Duke Hospital, I received a text alert. I pulled the phone from my shirt pocket, accidentally hitting the wrong button and causing the camera to flash.
"Are you trying to take a picture of me?" a woman in front of me asked hatefully. "Are you trying to upskirt me?"
I showed the woman the solid black image on the phone and explained I am inept using my phone. She continued questioning me.
Finally, I snapped: "You are flattering yourself to think someone would want to upskirt you!"
She threatened to call security; I threatened "the guys with the butterfly nets" to take her to the paranoia unit.

<u>February 25, 2011</u>

I am still laughing about my humbling shopping experience at Macy's in Greenville.

Lady: "I just love watching you in the morning."
Jay: "Thank you. I'm amazed how many people in the Upstate watch us."
Lady: "I think you're the best, Gordon. I just love Channel 4."
Jay: "Your Friend 4 loves you, too."

<u>October 20, 2014</u>

After learning Pope Francis is coming to the U.S. next year...

"Daddy, I want to be the pope when I grow up," Malachi informed me.

It's good to set your sights high," I replied without cracking a smile. "I'm sure the Vatican needs a comedian."

ABOUT THE AUTHOR

Jay Siltzer, News 13 morning anchor, joined WLOS-TV in Asheville, NC, in 1999.

He is in his 25th year in the news business. After co-anchoring morning news for News 13, he provides health stories for News 13 at 5 p.m.

Also a meteorologist, he completed the Broadcast Meteorology Program at Mississippi State University. He is a member of the American Meteorological Society and holds the AMS Seal of Approval for Television and the AMS Seal of Approval for Radio. Friends call him "Stormy" because outdoor conditions are often at their worst when he fills in at the weather desk.

A 1989 graduate of Lander University with a bachelor's degree in political science, he previously worked as a reporter for WVLT-TV in Knoxville, TN; WJHL-TV in Johnson City, TN; and The Index-Journal newspaper in Greenwood, SC.

When not working, he often shares his experiences as a cancer survivor with various groups. A widower, he lives in Hendersonville, NC, with his son, Malachi. They are active parishioners at Immaculate Conception Church and share their home with Caper, a destructive tabby cat.

CPSIA information can be obtained at www.ICGtesting.com
Printed in the USA
BVIW12n1904141116
467817BV00011B/105

* 9 7 8 1 5 1 7 5 6 9 9 8 3 *